TOOLS FOR CAREGIVERS

- **F&P LEVEL:** C
- **WORD COUNT:** 28
- **CURRICULUM CONNECTIONS:** animals, habitats, nature

Skills to Teach

- **HIGH-FREQUENCY WORDS:** a, has, have, I, in, it, see, they
- **CONTENT WORDS:** beak, birds, claws, eats, feathers, fly, live, parrot(s), pretty, trees, wings
- **PUNCTUATION:** exclamation points, periods
- **WORD STUDY:** /k/, spelled c (*claws*); long /e/, spelled ea (*beak, eats*); long /e/, spelled ee (*see, trees*); long /e/, spelled y (*pretty*); long /i/, spelled y (*fly*)
- **TEXT TYPE:** information report

Before Reading Activities

- Read the title and give a simple statement of the main idea.
- Have students "walk" through the book and talk about what they see in the pictures.
- Introduce new vocabulary by having students predict the first letter and locate the word in the text.
- Discuss any unfamiliar concepts that are in the text.

After Reading Activities

Talk with readers about the different sounds the letter y can make. It can make a long /e/ sound, like in the word *pretty*. It can also make a long /i/ sound, like in the word *fly*. Write both sounds and examples on the board. Ask readers to name and spell other words that use y as a long /e/ sound or as a long /i/ sound. Write their answers on the board.

Tadpole Books are published by Jump!, 5357 Penn Avenue South, Minneapolis, MN 55419, www.jumplibrary.com

Copyright ©2024 Jump. International copyright reserved in all countries. No part of this book may be reproduced in any form without written permission from the publisher.

Editor: Jenna Gleisner **Designer:** Emma Almgren-Bersie

Photo Credits: Tracy Starr/Shutterstock, cover, 2tr, 6–7; Eric Isselee/Shutterstock, 1; artiste9999/iStock, 2tl, 4–5; GlobalP/iStock, 2ml, 10–11; Ondrej Prosicky/Shutterstock, 2mr, 2br, 12–13, 16bl; Ogphoto/iStock, 2bl, 8–9; tracielouise/iStock, 3; Zeng Wei Jun/Shutterstock, 14–15; jsdeoliv/iStock, 16tl; naturelovephotography/iStock, 16tr; KAMONRAT/Shutterstock, 16br.

Library of Congress Cataloging-in-Publication Data
Names: Nilsen, Genevieve, author.
Title: Parrots / by Genevieve Nilsen.
Description: Minneapolis, MN: Jump!, Inc., (2024)
Series: My first animal books | Includes index.
Audience: Ages 3–6
Identifiers: LCCN 2022054044 (print)
LCCN 2022054045 (ebook)
ISBN 9798885246798 (hardcover)
ISBN 9798885246804 (paperback)
ISBN 9798885246811 (ebook)
Subjects: LCSH: Parrots—Juvenile literature.
Classification: LCC QL696.P7 N56 2024 (print)
LCC QL696.P7 (ebook)
DDC 598.7/1—dc23/eng/20221110
LC record available at https://lccn.loc.gov/2022054044
LC ebook record available at https://lccn.loc.gov/2022054045

MY FIRST ANIMAL BOOKS

PARROTS

by Genevieve Nilsen

TABLE OF CONTENTS

Words to Know	2
Parrots	3
Let's Review!	16
Index	16

WORDS TO KNOW

beak

claws

feathers

fly

trees

wings

PARROTS

I see a parrot!

It has a beak.

beak

It eats.

It has claws.

Parrots live in trees.

They have feathers.

They have wings.

wing

They fly!

Pretty birds!

LET'S REVIEW!

Parrots are birds. Their feathers can be many colors. What colors are these parrots?

INDEX

beak 4
claws 7
eats 5
feathers 11

fly 13
trees 9
wings 12